APARTHEID IN SOUTH AFRICA

SEAN CONNOLLY

www.heinemann.co.uk
Visit our website to find out more information about **Heinemann Library** books.

To order:
 Phone 44 (0) 1865 888066
 Send a fax to 44 (0) 1865 314091
 Visit the Heinemann Bookshop at www.heinemann.co.uk to browse our catalogue and order online.

First published in Great Britain by Heinemann Library, Halley Court, Jordan Hill, Oxford OX2 8EJ, a division of Reed Educational and Professional Publishing Ltd.
Heinemann is a registered trademark of Reed Educational and Professional Publishing Ltd.

OXFORD MELBOURNE AUCKLAND JOHANNESBURG BLANTYRE GABORONE IBADAN PORTSMOUTH (NH) USA CHICAGO

© Reed Educational and Professional Publishing Ltd 2001
The moral right of the proprietor has been asserted.

Designed by AMR
Illustrated by Chartwell Illustrators
Originated by Dot Gradations
Printed by South China Printers

05 04 03 02 01
10 9 8 7 6 5 4 3 2 1
ISBN 0 431 11860 4

British Library Cataloguing in Publication Data

Connolly, Sean
  Apartheid in South Africa. – (Troubled world)
  1.Apartheid – South Africa – Juvenile literature 2.South Africa – Politics and government – 20th century – Juvenile literature
  I.Title
  968'.05

Acknowledgements
The publishers would like to thank the following for permission to reproduce photographs:
Pg.4 Popperfoto/Reuters; Pg.7 Link/Greg English; Pg.8 Hulton Getty; Pg.11 AA Publishers; Pg.12 Corbis/Reuters; Pg.14 Hulton Deutsch; Pg.15 Hulton Getty; Pg.16 Hulton Getty; Pg.18 Hulton Getty; Pg.19 [left] Hulton Getty [right] Hulton Deutsch; Pg.21 Hulton Deutsch; Pg.23 African History Archive; Pg.24 Popperfoto; Pg.25 Hulton Getty; Pg.26 African History Archive; Pg.27 African History Archive; Pg.28 African History Archive; Pg.30 Keystone/Hulton; Pg.33 Hulton Getty; Pg.34 Topham Picturepoint; Pg.35 Hulton Getty; Pg.36 Africanet; Pg.38 Popperfoto; Pg.41 Camera Press; Pg.42 Hulton Getty; Pg.43 Camera Press; Pg.44 Frank Spooner/Gamma; Pg.46 Hulton Getty; Pg.47 Corbis/Charles O'Rear; Pg.49 IDAF; Pg.51 Popperfoto; Pg.52 Corbis/Peter Turnley; Pg.53 Popperfoto; Pg.54 Popperfoto; Pg.56 Popperfoto; Pg.59 Popperfoto.

Cover photograph reproduced with permission of Rex Features

Every effort has been made to contact copyright holders of any material reproduced in this book. Any omissions will be rectified in subsequent printings if notice is given to the publishers.

Contents

Words that appear in the text in bold, **like this**, are explained in the Glossary.

A rainbow nation

On 10 February 1990 an occurrence in South Africa captured the world's attention. Newspaper reporters and broadcasters alike devoted their energies to describing the enormous event that had changed the face of South Africa overnight – Nelson Mandela's release. Mandela had been imprisoned in 1964 for his active role in trying to overcome **apartheid**, a system of laws and regulations that for more than 40 years had imposed many restrictions on the majority of South Africans who were not white. He had become the most **potent** symbol of this struggle and over the course of time had become the most famous political prisoner in the world.

By the time of Mandela's release most elements of apartheid had been dismantled, but no-one – in South Africa or the world at large – believed that the change would be complete without his freedom. This book examines the system of apartheid and looks at the forces that led to its development, as well as the efforts of all the people whose sacrifices led to its downfall. But first it is worth looking at South Africa itself, in order to see how such a system could have been set in place.

Zulus, who form the largest black ethnic group in South Africa, recall their warrior past in their celebration dances.

Contrast and variety

South Africa lies at the southern tip of Africa, between the Atlantic Ocean to the west and the Indian Ocean to the east. It is nearly five times larger than the United Kingdom but has only about two thirds of the population. A large plateau, with average elevations of between 1500 and 2000 metres above sea level, covers most of the interior of the country. To the east this plateau rises to form the Drakensberg chain of mountains. This range acts as a 'rain shadow', causing any moisture-laden clouds from the Indian Ocean to deposit rain on their slopes. Between the Drakensberg chain and the ocean is a strip of well-watered land that was once covered with lush woodlands.

To the west along the plateau, the landscape is much drier. The comparative lack of rain means that the northern part of the plateau, called the high veld, can only support a **savannah** environment of grasslands and scrub vegetation. Things become drier and sandier still in the southwest, where the Karoo and Kalahari regions are semi-desert landscapes. The extreme southwest, however, receives winter rains from the Atlantic, creating a climate like that of California or the Mediterranean.

The effects of the two oceans, coupled with the high altitude of the interior, mean that temperatures never reach the extremes of other African countries. There are occasional droughts and even floods, but generally the climate is steady and predictable. These factors explain why agriculture can play such a large role in the economy, and South Africa produces large amounts of crops and meat. South African wines, produced in the Mediterranean-style southwest, are famous around the world.

A developed economy

In economic terms, South Africa has many advantages over other African countries. Living in a climate that never reaches the extremes of soaring temperatures or prolonged drought, its population never experiences the famines that have affected the Horn of Africa in the 1980s and again in 2000. Such famines not only take a toll on human life, but they also drain national economies of resources and potential.

In fact it is through **exploiting** its abundant natural resources that South Africa has developed. The fertile coastal strips support a buoyant agricultural sector, while the grasslands of the high veld are suited to large-scale livestock raising. Mining accounts for nearly 40 per cent of national export earnings. South Africa is the world's leading producer of gold, with annual extraction representing more than one-quarter of the world total. It is also the fifth largest producer of diamonds, including nearly 10 per cent of the world's quality gemstones.

In addition to the economic contributions of agriculture and mining, South Africa has – in comparison with other African countries – a diverse manufacturing sector. The banking and financial services industries are also well developed.

Factfile – South Africa in 2000

Full country name:	The Republic of South Africa
Area:	1,221,040 sq km
Population:	40.6 million
People:	76.1% black, 12.8% white (60% of whites are of Afrikaner descent, most of the rest are of British descent), 8.5% mixed race, 2.6% Indian/Asian descent.
Capital city:	Pretoria
Main languages:	English, Afrikaans, seSotho, isiXhosa, isiZulu
Religions:	Christian, Muslim, Hindu, Jewish and traditional religions
Government:	Party in power is the African National Congress (ANC)
President:	Thabo Mbeki

Human wealth

South Africa has earned the nickname 'the rainbow nation' on account of its diverse population, which comprises many races and ethnic groups. Black Africans constitute 76.1 per cent of the population, 12.8 per cent are whites, 8.5 per cent are coloureds (people of African and white heritage) and 2.6 per cent are Asians. The blacks belong to nine ethnic groups: Zulu, Xhosa, Pedi, Sotho, Tswana, Tsonga, Swazi, Ndebele and Venda. The Zulu are the largest of these groups, making up about 22 per cent of the total population. Whites are descended primarily from British, Dutch, German, and French Huguenot (Protestant) settlers.

It is this rich diversity that offers South Africa hope for the future, but it also lay at the root of the conflict and stagnation of the past. Modern South Africa is still feeling the legacy of centuries of oppression and **discrimination** against the majority of its population. Inequalities in wealth, which are evident in other countries with well-developed economies, are made worse by a legacy which denied most people the chance to own land, vote or even live where they chose in South Africa.

For decades South Africa was even divided along sporting lines, with rugby the preserve of the white – mainly Afrikaner – population.

Roots of division

South Africa is one of the oldest countries in the world, in terms of human habitation. Fossils of some of the earliest human ancestors have been uncovered there, as well as some of the oldest evidence of modern humans *(Homo sapiens)*. This evidence shows that for many thousands of years the people living in what is now South Africa lived by gathering nuts and roots, by gathering shellfish on the coast and by hunting antelope and other game on the grassy central plateau.

Waves of newcomers arrived in the area, in a process that continues to this day. Some of the different groups can be identified by languages spoken today as well as by the archaeological evidence of how they lived.

By about 2000 years ago there were three main groups of people living in the area. One group, known as the San people or sometimes as Bushmen, lived as hunter-gatherers. A second group of people, the Khoikhoi, herded sheep and cattle. The third major element, collectively known as Bantu because of their language group, cultivated crops such as sorghum, millet, melons and pumpkins.

Khoikhoi people still use ostrich eggs as water-storage bottles in the desert regions of South Africa.

With their more stable social units, the Khoikhoi and Bantu people came to dominate most of the South African region, with the San people forced to live in areas that could not support either livestock or crops.

The first Europeans

Life in South Africa for the first inhabitants was locally based with people owing **allegiance** to a chief, who in turn had to inspire loyalty to maintain his source of power. There was little contact with people living north of the Limpopo River and the active maritime trade on the Indian Ocean did not extend south of modern-day Mozambique.

By the beginning of the 16th century, however, the picture had become very different. Europeans had begun to round the Cape of Good Hope on their way east to Asia, and had made landfalls along the South African coast. The Portuguese were the first, but they used South Africa simply as a springboard for easterly navigation. The Dutch, though, found it very useful to establish a permanent base along the southern African coast, to act as a base for their own trading efforts in India and Java. In 1652 Jan van Riebeeck established a permanent settlement at Table Bay, near present-day Cape Town at the southern tip of Africa.

At first the Dutch thought that they could use the settlement to trade with local Khoikhoi people for meat, vegetables and other goods necessary to supply their Asia-bound sailors. But when the local people proved unwilling to co-operate with this plan, the Dutch decided to turn the settlement into a full-scale **colony**.

They took Khoikhoi land by force and began to fill the new colony with a variety of settlers. White settlers, either Dutch immigrants or Huguenots fleeing **persecution** in France, received pieces of land on which to establish farms. In order to work these farms, the new settlers brought in thousands of slaves from Indonesia, India, Madagascar and eastern Africa. The Dutch language that they spoke was influenced and shaped by elements from these different groups and became known as Afrikaans – and those who spoke it were called Afrikaners. These people are also referred to as Boers.

'What are you doing on my land? You have taken all the places where the eland and other game live. Why did you not stay where the sun goes down, where you came from?'
Koerikei, a San leader, addressing white farmers in the 1770s

The Dutch **colony** thrived and expanded, with more and more Khoikhoi land being taken as the white population doubled with each generation. Any raids on the new farms by the Khoikhoi were crushed.

Colonial conflict

Great Britain saw the importance of the Cape Colony and gained control of it from the Dutch in 1806. It formally became a British colony in 1814. The British instituted various reforms, including the abolition of slavery in 1833, but they also fought several wars of conquest against the local Xhosa people. Meanwhile the British also encountered **antagonism** from the Afrikaners, who felt increasingly oppressed under various aspects of British rule – especially the abolition of slavery.

In 1835 many Afrikaners, with the aim of escaping British oppression and recovering their own identity and **autonomy**, began the Great Trek. They eventually established two republics: the Orange Free State, north of the Orange River; and the South African Republic, located further north, in the Transvaal region. Diamonds were discovered in 1867 in Griqualand West (then part of the Transvaal), and this heightened hostility between the Afrikaners and the British. The Cape Colony **annexed** Griqualand West in 1871. The next year the Cape Colony was granted limited self-government by the British government. In 1877 the colony annexed the entire South African Republic but withdrew in 1881 after meeting fierce Afrikaner resistance. Cecil Rhodes became prime minister of the Cape Colony in 1890, and relations between the British and the Afrikaners deteriorated yet again. Rhodes resigned in 1896; three years later the Boer War began.

The Great Trek of the 1830s is commemorated in a giant monument in Johannesburg.

Biography – Paul Kruger

Stephanus Johannes Paulus Kruger (1825–1904) was born in Colesburg, in what was then called the Cape Colony. He went with his parents on the Great Trek to settle in the territory of the Transvaal, north of the Orange River. In the late 1850s these Transvaal territories united to form the South African Republic. Kruger had spent years fighting against the Zulu and other Africans who opposed the Afrikaner settlers. These experiences led to his election as commandant general of the Transvaal forces in 1864.

Kruger was one of the military leaders of the Afrikaners in the Transvaal who rebelled against the British forces in 1880. In the following year he helped negotiate the peace agreement with Great Britain and in 1883 was elected president of the South African Republic. In 1886 gold was discovered in the Transvaal, and the British flooded into the area. The Afrikaners resented the intrusion, and in retaliation Kruger's government passed severe voting restrictions and imposed high railway **tariffs**. This stance helped trigger the Boer War in 1899. During the Boer War, Kruger, who was by now too old to fight, went to Europe to try to convince various Continental powers to aid the South African Republic. After the defeat of the Afrikaners in 1902, Kruger settled in Europe.

Turning point: The modern state

The Boer War lasted from 1899 to 1902. The British military force of 200,000 soldiers was equal to roughly two-thirds of the entire Afrikaner population. The Afrikaners, more accustomed to the terrain and harsh conditions, fought a **guerrilla** campaign and scored several decisive victories over the British. The British responded by **interning** thousands of Afrikaners in **concentration camps**; 26,000 Afrikaners died in these camps, increasing anti-British hostility among the Afrikaner population. During the war, the British gained control over the Transvaal and the Orange Free State, which became crown **colonies**. They joined the Cape Colony and Natal, which had already been under British control.

In 1910 the four British colonies in South Africa united as the Union of South Africa under the terms of the South Africa Act. The British, however, knew that peace in this newly unified country would not last long without the co-operation of the Afrikaners. Several years of hard bargaining between the British and the Afrikaners had smoothed out some of the differences between the four colonies, and in doing so had established a framework for white rule overall.

Many black South Africans joined the British army to fight against the Afrikaners during the Boer War.

'Your cattle are gone, my countrymen,
Go rescue them! Go rescue them!
Leave the **breechloader** alone
And turn to the pen.
Take paper and ink,
For that is your shield.'
**The Xhosa poet, I W W Citashe, writing just before
Union in 1910**

The ballot box

One of the most important features of this new agreement
concerned the **franchise**, or regulations about who would be
allowed to vote. The four colonies had made it either illegal (in
the Afrikaner republics) or virtually impossible (in the British
colonies) for non-whites to be allowed to vote legally. The new
system maintained these differences, which theoretically allowed
some land-owning blacks to vote in the Cape and Natal. Still,
only white males could become Members of Parliament.

The black population did not welcome the set of voting
regulations that underpinned the new unity. Most of their
protests were concentrated in the Cape, where there was a
western-educated **elite**. The Cape also had a large coloured
population, which had also come to expect better things from
British rule. These two groups aired their views in local
newspapers and even sent a delegation to London to **petition**
the British Parliament against passing the South Africa Act. Their
actions had no effect, and the Act was passed in May 1910. Four
months later, the first South African general elections were held.
Louis Botha, who had commanded Afrikaner forces in the Boer
War, was elected prime minister.

Birth of a nation

The South Africa that Botha governed had just under six million
inhabitants. About two-thirds were considered to be black, or of
full African descent. The next largest group was the white
population, making up about one-fifth. Next came the 'coloured'
population – people of mixed white and African backgrounds –
who accounted for one-tenth of the overall population. Less
than three per cent of the population were Asian, mainly people
descended from Indians who the British had brought in to work
as farm labourers and on the plantations.

South Africa's Asian minority played a major role in the struggle for racial equality in their adopted country throughout the 20th century.

The Indian population, although statistically small, would play an important part in the long struggle to end the white domination of South African politics. At the time of Union in 1910 one of its leading members was Mohandas Karamchand Gandhi, who had been born in India and trained as a lawyer in Britain. Gandhi, who later became associated with Indian independence, had spent years campaigning for wider civil rights for South Africa's Indian population. During the Boer War, Gandhi organized an ambulance corps for the British army and commanded a Red Cross unit. After the war he returned to his campaign for Indian rights. In 1910, he founded Tolstoy Farm, near Johannesburg, a co-operative settlement for Indians.

Gandhi also had links with the Indian National Congress, a political organization that pressed for the **autonomy** and independence of India itself. The Indian National Congress urged its members and supporters to adopt a strategy of 'non-violent resistance' to unjust laws in India, so that the British would eventually have to recognize their demands. The discipline and aims of the Indian National Congress impressed many black and coloured South Africans, and the organization would become an important influence on the struggle for South African rights.

Mining

The discovery of diamonds attracted hundreds of would-be millionaires to the area around Griqualand West in the 1870s. The town of Kimberley developed around this new diamond-mining industry and within several years had become the second largest settlement in Southern Africa.

Whites owned the mines and had all the skilled jobs, but they needed thousands of black labourers to perform a wide range of unskilled – and often dangerous – tasks. Although wages were low for these workers, black labourers arrived in great numbers. Nearly all were male, and had left their families behind in other parts of the country. Mine owners housed them in strictly controlled closed barracks, known as compounds. Workers were only allowed out of the compounds to work the mines.

A similar pattern of labour emerged in the mid-1800s, when gold was discovered in the Transvaal region. The city of Johannesburg developed in this gold-mining region. The system of harsh discipline within the compounds – with random searches and passes needed for any movement – would later become the basis for the laws and regulations that underpinned the **apartheid** system.

The working day was long and difficult for black labourers at the Republic Gold Mining Company in the 1880s.

Positions harden

South Africa in 1910 had evolved into a political whole, although there were divisions running through the entire framework of unity. The most fundamental source of division was between the ruling white minority and the non-white – mainly black – majority, which had few rights in the new country. Many blacks had either bought land outright or had **squatted** on land in the Transvaal and the Orange Free State, when the mining boom had made these areas attractive. Moreover, many black South Africans had fought in the Boer War (mainly on the British side) and still had firearms. The prospect of an armed, land-owning black population filled many white South Africans with fear. There was talk of the white population being 'swamped in a sea of black faces', and many whites saw Botha's primarily Afrikaner government as being too weak in the face of that threat.

Blacks, on the other hand, had seen the inequalities and **discrimination** of the 19th century carried over to the new century and given legal backing within the new government. They foresaw – accurately – that the white rulers would make life even more difficult for them, and that the only way for the existing system to survive was through strengthening the position of whites even further.

Prime Minister Louis Botha maintained a military bearing throughout his years in politics.

New organizations

The educated leadership of the black population, which had failed to stop the passing of the South Africa Act, still believed in pressing their claims through **constitutional** methods. In 1912 they gathered in Bloemfontein, Orange Free State, to form an organization to represent them. The name they chose for this organization, the South African Native National Congress (SANNC), reflected their ambition to **emulate** the Indian National Congress, which was the leading anti-colonial group in the British Empire. (Thirteen years later it would change its name to the African National Congress, or ANC.)

The SANNC at this stage was resolutely non-violent, and aimed to further its ends with **petitions** and occasional peaceful demonstrations. It had no real influence on the government, but from the start it was an important means of airing the various strands of African opinion. Some of these strands would later become impatient with what they saw as the meek attitude of the organization.

Discontent and defection

There were also voices raised within the white population, this time among Afrikaners who felt that the new government was too moderate in its treatment of blacks and that the Afrikaners did not have enough economic or political power. Resentment turned into near revolt in 1914. Prime Minister Botha pledged full South African support for Britain in the First World War. One Afrikaner general defected with his troops to neighbouring German South West Africa. Other Afrikaners in the Transvaal rose up briefly against the government. Botha succeeded in defeating South West Africa (which would become a virtual South African **colony** until it became independent as Namibia).

A greater threat to Botha's 'moderate', pro-British stance came from J B M Hertzog, who had also served as an Afrikaner general in the Boer War. Hertzog had served in Botha's first **cabinet** and was also a member of the South African Party. By 1914, however, he became a focal point of Afrikaner discontent and formed the National Party. It was under the leadership of this party that the philosophy of **apartheid** in South Africa would later become government policy.

Natives Land Act

If the harsh conditions imposed on black mine-workers were signals of subsequent social control under the **apartheid** system, then one of the first Acts of the 1910 government paved the way for later inequalities in land distribution. Many blacks had **squatted** on – or bought – land in mining regions in the 1800s. Under the Natives Land Act of 1913 (later renamed the Black Land Act) they were forced off these valuable lands. In compensation they were offered 'reserves', specially designated for black populations. The amount of land set aside for these reserves was insultingly small – only 7.3 per cent of South Africa. The remaining 92.7 per cent, including all the productive farming and mining areas, was reserved for whites. Lines were drawn on the map of South Africa, clearly separating black African reserves from white farming areas. Africans could no longer purchase land in white areas. In addition, it became illegal for them even to farm on white-owned land and pay the owners in the system known as **share-cropping**.

Vast numbers of black men were drawn to Johannesburg and other mining centres at the end of the 19th century.

Uneasy alliance

Louis Botha died in 1919 and was succeeded by another pro-British Afrikaner, Jan Christiaan Smuts. Like Botha, Smuts had commanded troops against the British during the Boer War, so once more there seemed hope for **reconciliation** with the National Party. But Smuts was preoccupied with economic problems, including a fall in the price of gold. Hertzog's National Party, in alliance with the smaller Labour Party (also anti-black) defeated Smuts in the 1924 general election.

Jan Christiaan Smuts (left) and J B M Hertzog (below).

'I am not one of those who always have their mouths full of reconciliation ... [South Africa] can no longer be governed by non-Afrikaners, by people who do not have the right love for South Africa.'
J B M Hertzog, during the 1924 general election campaign

Hertzog would remain Prime Minister until 1939 but during the Depression of the 1930s he agreed to become dual leader (with Smuts) of the United Party, in order to prompt economic recovery. The two represented very different approaches on nearly every important issue and the alliance was shaky at best. It fell apart in 1939, when Britain declared war on Germany. Hertzog tried to keep South Africa neutral, but he was defeated in Parliament. Smuts once more became Prime Minister.

Turning point: Apartheid enshrined

The British Act that established the Union of South Africa in 1910 had granted **dominion** status to the country. South Africa's government was based on the British parliamentary system, and the country remained within the framework of the British Empire. In this respect, South Africa resembled Australia, New Zealand and Canada, which were also British dominions.

The dramatic events in Europe, highlighted by Britain's declaration of war against Germany, had brought South Africa's relationship with Britain into sharp relief. Hertzog's failed attempt to pass a motion declaring South Africa's neutrality in the Second World War would normally have led to a general election. The governor-general, representing the British monarch, believed that such an election would endanger Britain's ability to rely on South Africa in the war effort, so he invited General Smuts to form a new United Party government. Smuts led South Africa into the war, on the side of Britain and the Allies. Once more, Afrikaner opinion was inflamed by being forced to side with the former enemy. The sense of resentment was to continue even after the Allied victory in 1945.

Postwar upheaval

The British were very grateful for South Africa's involvement in the war, and Smuts began to be considered something of a world statesman. Events at home were beginning to dent that reputation. In a sense, Smuts failed to notice how his own position owed so much to the British, a position that distanced himself from Afrikaner opinion. The Afrikaners, for the most part, wanted to minimize such British connections and to take an even stronger role in governing the country.

There were also deep-seated and growing feelings of discontent aroused among the non-white population at this time. The majority of South Africans were inspired by the anti-colonial sentiments that were developing on the world scene in the aftermath of the war. Non-white South Africans could look to other countries in Africa and Asia to see how similar majority populations were opposing their colonial rulers. Seeing the parallels with their own country, many blacks began to argue for a more active opposition to the policies of the South African government. These opinions would prove crucial to the direction the country would take.

Renewed activism

By the mid-1940s black **activism** was channelled through two organizations, both of which worried the white government greatly. The first was the African National Congress (ANC), which was previously called the SANNC. The ANC had been relatively quiet in the 1930s, its leadership divided on the best methods to press for social change. In the years after the war, however, it became more active, reflecting the sense of impatience and discontent in the **squatter** camps that surrounded Johannesburg and some other cities. The ANC moved to end the social segregation in South African society with activities such as the bus **boycotts** in Alexandra, Johannesburg and Brakpan in the East Rand.

Boycotts as a weapon

Africans adopted the tactic of a boycott as a means of improving their living conditions, however slightly. The word boycott comes from Charles Boycott, a 19th-century British land representative in Ireland. Poor Irish tenants, appalled by Boycott's harsh measures, refused to work on his lands and isolated him in every way possible. Africans used this method effectively in the 1940s, when they refused to ride on township buses after fares increased. Thousands of people marched in support of the boycott, which achieved its aim – fares were reduced.

Violent riots in South African mines led to deaths and injuries in the 1940s.

The second organization was the South African **Communist** Party, which had been established in 1920. The Communist Party had been founded to promote the interests of the white working class, but during the 1930s it had also become divided – on the issue of loyalty to Moscow, the 'capital' of communism. Things changed in 1936, when it moved its headquarters to Cape Town and began to concentrate on improving working conditions for all South Africans – white and black alike.

Like the ANC, the Communist Party had become a force to be reckoned with by the mid-1940s. It was particularly successful in mobilizing support among black workers in the gold-mining industry, which was crucial to the country's economy. In August 1946 it supported a **strike** by these workers, calling for a wage increase and for better food. Between 60,000 and 70,000 workers joined the strike before it was crushed by the government – twelve people were killed.

The crucial election

Afrikaner resentment and fears, heightened by the new confidence of the non-white population, set the stage for the 1948 general election in South Africa. Voters had the choice between the governing United Party of Smuts and an alliance of the small Afrikaner Party and the National Party of Dr D F Malan, who had succeeded Hertzog. The National Party played directly to white fears and one of the Afrikaans phrases that kept cropping up in their campaign was *swart gevaar*, meaning 'black danger'. The tactic worked, and on 26 May 1948 the National Party was elected to govern South Africa. The victory enabled the party to put into practice the other – and more famous – Afrikaans election term: **apartheid**, or 'separateness'.

Right from the start, the 'National' of the National Party had meant not the nation of South Africa, or even that of white South Africa, but of the Afrikaner people living there. The party's first moves after winning the 1948 election were to strengthen the Afrikaner position. Sensing that English-speaking South Africans would either weaken or oppose apartheid, the National Party altered the borders of many voting **constituencies** to ensure that the party would hold on to power in future elections. That move cleared the way for the real task ahead – setting in place the system of apartheid itself.

Biography – Daniel Malan, the 'architect of apartheid'

Daniel François Malan (1874–1959) was born in Riebeek West (in what is now Western Cape province). Following the deeply religious tradition of his Afrikaner family, Malan became a minister in the Reformed Churches. During the First World War he became the first editor of *De Burger*, the most powerful Afrikaans nationalist newspaper in the Cape region. Malan used religious arguments to claim that Afrikaners, unlike English-speaking South Africans, were a *natie* (nation) and a *volk* (a people). Elected to parliament in 1918, he rose to **cabinet** rank in 1924 and established himself as a senior member of the National Party. In 1940, after Hertzog's parliamentary defeat on neutrality, Malan assumed leadership of the National Party, achieving victory in the 1948 general election. During his six years as prime minister Malan was able to implement racial policies with a body of **legislation** that became known as apartheid. Malan retired in 1954 and was replaced by J G Strijdom.

Daniel François Malan had careers as a clergyman and journalist before turning to politics.

> 'The choice before us is one of these two divergent courses: either that of integration, which in the long run would amount to national suicide on the part of the whites; or that of **apartheid**, which professes to safeguard the future of every race.'
> **Part of the National Party's 'Race Relations' proposals for the 1948 election**

The new system at work

The Afrikaner people have always been deeply religious, and most belong to a strict Protestant denomination called the Dutch Reformed Church. The National Party of 1948 used religious arguments as well as political ones to justify the separation of races within South Africa. It believed that the different races living together – and most importantly, intermarrying – was immoral. Nevertheless, only the most extreme believers in apartheid thought that all blacks could be removed from every white area. Many white employers, both in cities and on farms, had come to rely on cheap black labour.

The new system of apartheid had to find a balance between racial separation and allowing such labour to continue. Rather than seeing the country composed of a ruling white minority and a non-white majority, the National Party viewed the black population as belonging to different 'tribes': each of these tribes, like the whites, was a minority and should live on its own tribal land. The National Party also saw it as its religious duty to root out **communism**, a system of beliefs that it interpreted widely to include a range of 'unacceptable' behaviour.

Petty rules about racial division affected every aspect of life in South Africa during the apartheid era.

Legislation passed in the late 1940s and early 1950s formed the basic framework of apartheid. The Mixed Marriages Act (1949) and the Immorality Act (1950) outlawed sexual relations between members of different racial groups. These acts, coupled with the Population Registration Act (1950), strictly defined each person's race. The new legislation also led to absurd 'reclassifications' of some people, even within families. The Group Areas Act (1950), backed by later legislation, led to designated areas being set aside for each of the four main racial groups: Europeans (whites), Bantu (blacks), Coloureds (mixed race) and Asians. The subsequent legislation concentrated on creating 'homelands' for each of the ten black 'tribes'. The homelands, also known as **Bantustans**, were Bophuthatswana, Ciskei, Gazankulu, KaNgwane, KwaNdebele, KwaZulu, Lebowa, Qwaqwa, Transkei and Venda. All blacks were considered to be citizens of these Bantustans, rather than of South Africa, and, under the Pass Laws, they needed to carry passes in order to enter white areas.

Armed patrols would stop blacks to make sure they had the passes required to enter white areas.

Communist activities

The Suppression of Communism Act (1950) declared the Communist Party to be an illegal organization, and any organization or individual promoting 'communist activities' was similarly declared illegal. In line with **Cold War** international politics, the National Party declared 'communist activities' to include arguing for world peace, international trade union solidarity or the end of colonialism.

Resistance grows

The African National Congress, which had been established as a means of promoting the black cause in South Africa, had languished during most of the 1920s and 1930s. Its pleas and **petitions** to successive governments had gone largely unheeded, and many younger members were impatient for change. Some of these younger members, including Walter Sisulu, Oliver Tambo and Nelson Mandela, had received good educations through the small network of **missionary** schools within South Africa. These schools, as well as the University of Fort Hare, offered the only route to educational advancement for black South Africans.

Nelson Mandela and Oliver Tambo worked hard to ease the legal problems of black South Africans.

In 1944 a group of young ANC members, including Mandela, established the Youth League as a way of attracting young and committed people to the ANC. Their efforts – coupled with the higher profile that the ANC took in **strikes** and demonstrations – were already bearing fruit by the time the National Party gained power in 1948. And curiously it was through some of the new **apartheid**-related laws that the ANC became even more prominent.

The Population Registration Act, for example, had worsened the position of the coloured population, based mainly in the Cape. For many years considered 'almost white' and given leeway in terms of jobs and education, this group now began to suffer from legal **discrimination**. Many coloured people became attracted to the black cause and joined the ANC as a result. Likewise, the banning of the **Communist** Party meant that many of their **activists** saw the ANC as the only means of promoting social change. As with the coloureds, the communists brought many well-educated and experienced activists with them into the ANC.

The Programme of Action

In 1949 the ANC announced its Programme of Action, which Mandela, Tambo and Sisulu helped draw up. The Programme called for the ANC to use the weapons of strikes, **boycotts** and **civil disobedience**. The main demands were that all South Africans have equal rights as citizens, in education, **parliamentary representation**, property ownership and work. And unlike most previous ANC documents it presented its aims as a series of demands rather than requests.

Albert Luthuli, a powerful anti-apartheid activist became president of the ANC in 1952. That same year the ANC launched its Campaign for the Defiance of Unjust Laws. Again, Mandela played an important role, this time as National Volunteer-in-Chief. This post meant that he travelled around South Africa persuading ordinary people to defy the harsh apartheid laws. For his part in this campaign Mandela and others were arrested and convicted under the Suppression of Communism Act. The judge, however, agreed that the men had not encouraged people to use violence, so they got only a two year **suspended sentence**.

Such high-profile actions contributed greatly to the ANC cause. In the following years there were similar acts of defiance – sometimes accounting for little more than walking about after an 11 pm curfew – followed by similar punishments. And although leaders such as Mandela and Sisulu found their own lives becoming more limited by government **banning orders**, the message spread throughout the country. Instead of relying on its leaders to make pleas to the government the ANC was encouraging the public to join the movement and to take direct action.

Walter Sisulu's forceful speeches drew many – including Nelson Mandela – to the struggle against apartheid.

Freedom and treason

Apartheid by now was becoming an international issue, and the United Nations set up a special commission to examine racial **discrimination** in South Africa. Prime Minister Malan refused to co-operate with this commission, but the international concern inspired many South Africans who opposed apartheid. In April 1955, a group of 3000 South Africans from all racial and ethnic backgrounds gathered at the Congress of the People, near Johannesburg, to draft the Freedom Charter. It called for a non-racial, unified and **democratic** South Africa. The ANC adopted the charter as its basic statement.

The government saw itself on the defensive and began to take decisive steps to root out opposition. In 1956 some 156 anti-apartheid **activists**, including prominent members of the ANC leadership such as Mandela, were arrested and charged with treason. The trial, which was to last until 1961, was the longest in South African history. Mandela, the most prominent and eloquent of the accused, was able to show that the ANC was not opposing whites, but only **white supremacy**. During the course of the trial he established himself as the ANC's chief asset – and the government's most skilful adversary.

Nelson Mandela (third from left) and the other 1956 Treason Trial defendants knew that their trial would shape public opinion about apartheid.

Biography – Nelson Mandela

Nelson Mandela was well placed to become a prominent statesman for the ANC and South Africa as a whole. He was born in 1918 as the son of a Thembu tribal chief in Umtata, in what is now the province of Eastern Cape. His name at birth, Rolihlahla, means 'pulling the branch of the tree' in the Xhosa language. He was named 'Nelson' by a teacher when he was a small boy.

Mandela was related to royal family of the Thembu people who lived in that part of South Africa. This connection meant that after his father's death, Nelson became an adoptive son of the royal family and received many of the advantages that members of the immediate family enjoyed. Most important of these was the chance to receive a good education, something that was denied nearly every other young black South African.

Mandela was expelled from the University of Fort Hare and moved to Johannesburg, where he met Walter Sisulu and other prominent members of the ANC. Sisulu persuaded Mandela to continue his education by studying at night, and through the 1940s Mandela worked days in law offices and spent nights either in ANC activities or completing his course to become a lawyer. Nelson put his time to good use and achieved all the qualifications needed to practise law. In 1952 he and Oliver Tambo opened their own legal office in Johannesburg. The two lawyers tried to help their clients – most of whom were also non-whites – in their struggle against the apartheid laws. Nelson's knowledge of the law enabled him to argue the ANC's case persuasively in the 1956–1961 Treason Trial and later in the 1963– 1964 trial that would lead to his famous prison sentence.

'We the people of South Africa, black and white together equals, countrymen and brothers adopt this Freedom Charter; and we pledge ourselves to strive together, sparing neither strength nor courage, until the democratic changes here set out have been won.'
An extract from the Freedom Charter, agreed on 26 June 1955

Turning point: Sharpeville

By the mid-1950s, at about the time that the famous Treason Trial was beginning, the South African government began to feel threatened. The **banning orders** on anti-**apartheid** leaders, coupled with the free publicity that the Treason Trial seemed to be giving to the ANC cause, seemed only to strengthen the forces ranged against apartheid.

The government was, in fact, echoing the concerns of the Afrikaner people. In 1955, the South African parliament passed a motion to appoint six new Supreme Court judges to hear questions relating to the country's constitution. With the inclusion of the new, more pro-apartheid judges, one of the few brakes against apartheid had been removed.

By the 1950s many white South Africans held public demonstrations to protest against the voting injustices inflicted under apartheid.

Strijdom led the National Party to a general election victory in 1958 but died soon afterwards. He was replaced by the Dutch-born Dr Henrik Verwoerd, who had played an important role in formulating essential apartheid **legislation** after the 1948 victory.

At that time, Verwoerd understood some of the basic dilemmas of apartheid – notably the need for a pool of cheap black labour within the restricted white areas – but he had skilfully imposed layer upon layer of restrictions on any black people who did live or work within such areas.

Now, with the legislative groundwork laid and judicial restrictions largely removed, he was in a position to strengthen apartheid. Verwoerd's plans, sometimes called 'grand apartheid', called for even greater state control in areas such as education, employment and social life.

Black divisions

Verwoerd and other members of the government were relieved to see that there were tensions within the black community. Armed police had broken up the Congress of the People in 1955, but at the time the government seemed to have lost the real battle. The Freedom Charter was the evidence of this defeat, but the same Congress exposed a serious rift within the anti-apartheid movement.

Many of the black members came from Transvaal or Free State, areas that were harder hit by harsh racial **discrimination** than most of South Africa. The formative experiences of these members had been far more brutal than those of blacks in, for example, the Cape. As a result they had come to distrust any whites, whether they be government officials, Christian **missionaries** or even **communist** union officials. In the view of these black members, native African people had to formulate their own future, removed from the influence of white people, however well intentioned. By 1958 their views had hardened enough for them to break away from the ANC to form the Pan-African Congress (PAC). Membership of the PAC was limited to blacks and there was a strong emphasis on self-reliance.

Sharpeville

Ever since the days of the first diamond and gold mines in the 1800s, black South Africans had flocked to the major mining centres and cities in search of work. Those who were not housed directly in compounds usually lived in all-black suburbs, or 'townships', around the cities. Even after the formulation of **apartheid** the government understood the need for such separate living areas for blacks, and the townships seemed to provide the answer.

Sharpeville, located about 80 kilometres (50 miles) south of Johannesburg, was a 'model' township. Construction on it began in 1942 and by the late 1950s it had running water and good sanitation – conditions that were lacking in the township it replaced. Then the government began to move people forcibly from the old township to the new one. Those who refused to move, on the grounds that they could not afford the higher rents, were evicted to 'reserves'. This led to a tense atmosphere, which was made worse by the chronic unemployment among the young people.

On 21 March 1960 the PAC organized a 5000-strong protest against the Pass Laws (see page 25) outside the Sharpeville police station. The police tried to disperse them from behind a wire fence, but the protesters stayed put for many hours. Finally a scuffle broke out, and the police panicked and began to fire into the crowd. The protestors ran for safety but the shooting continued. In the end, 69 people were killed and 180 were wounded. Nearly everyone had been shot in the back.

Stunned reactions

The world was stunned by the news of the massacre that had occurred in Sharpeville. Many people had little knowledge about South Africa, or its brutal social system. Many of those that did, knew of apartheid only in the abstract sense that laws and regulations made life difficult for the majority of South Africans. Now it became clear that violence underpinned the system.

Within South Africa the reaction quickly moved from stunned disbelief to outright fury. Similar anti-government demonstrations continued although many people were put off by the prospect of bloodshed. The government, for its part, declared a **State of Emergency** in late March and on 6 April it banned both the ANC and the PAC.

The response of these two organizations was to go underground and to begin a campaign of military resistance. The ANC founded a military wing, Umkonto we Sizwe ('Spear of the Nation'), with Nelson Mandela as its commander-in-chief. The PAC's military wing was called Poqo, meaning 'pure'. They embarked on a campaign of **sabotage** and Poqo also assassinated some chiefs in Transkei and Ciskei whom they accused of collaborating with the government.

Gone were the days of passive resistance, **petitions** to the government and other measures inspired by the non-violent preaching of Gandhi. In a sense, the aftermath of Sharpeville was to bring about a state of **civil war** in South Africa.

This famous photograph of the Sharpeville massacre appeared in newapapers around the world, providing powerful evidence of the cruelty and injustice of the apartheid system.

The international profile

International protests rained down on the South African government, notably from fellow members of the **Commonwealth**, the grouping of former British **colonies**. The attitude of the government was defiant. On 5 October South Africans voted to leave the Commonwealth and to establish a republic. Two weeks later, Verwoerd's National Party was returned to power in a general election.

Mandela was acquitted in his long-running Treason Trial in 1961, but with his new role as commander-in-chief of the military wing of the ANC – Umkonto we Sizwe, also called the MK, knew that his every move was being monitored by the government. He then went 'on the run', travelling around South Africa in a number of disguises, staying at safe houses and urging people to take part in the struggle against **apartheid**. Mandela was extremely successful in this role, in which he adopted the clothes and mannerisms of lowly labourers and chauffeurs. He relished the difficulties that the police had in tracing him, taunting them and the government in a series of signed letters to newspapers. This dangerous game of cat-and-mouse earned Mandela the nickname 'the Black Pimpernel', a reference to the hero of the novel *The Scarlet Pimpernel* by Baroness Emma Orczy, set in the turbulent years of the French Revolution.

The decision by white South African voters to establish a republic reflected their defiance of international opinion.

Dr Kwame's leadership of an independent Ghana inspired Nelson Mandela and other high-ranking ANC members.

In 1961 Mandela and Oliver Tambo left the country secretly to gain support from newly independent African countries and from sympathetic followers in Britain. While they were on this secret mission, Albert Luthuli was awarded the Nobel Prize for Peace, which helped their cause further. Mandela returned to South Africa in 1962, but Tambo remained abroad as the ANC President-in-absence. A network of communication kept Tambo in touch with ANC leaders within South Africa, enabling him to gauge the mood of the people and to formulate strategy. At the same time, MK soldiers would be trained in exile outside South Africa before infiltrating back in to carry out works of **sabotage**. This arrangement proved to be successful, and lasted for three decades.

'I recognize ... that in my country, South Africa, the spirit of peace is subject to some of the severest tensions known to man. For that reason South Africa has been and continues to be in the focus of world attention. I therefore regard this award as a recognition of the sacrifices by my people of all races, particularly the African people, who have endured and suffered so much for so long.'
Albert Luthuli, on receiving the Nobel Peace Prize in 1961

Turning point: the ANC on trial

Soon after Nelson Mandela's secret return to South Africa in 1962 he met other ANC leaders at Liliesleaf Farm in Rivonia, a rural suburb of Johannesburg. The farm was an unofficial headquarters where ANC leaders planned strategy. While on his travels Mandela had undergone military training in Algeria; back in South Africa he was keen to link his recent experiences with the ANC's overall planning.

Events, however, would mean that the ANC would soon suffer a terrible blow. The South African police had not relented in their attempts to locate Mandela; spies and informers had told them of Mandela's general movements and of the ANC's strategic planning sessions. On the night of 5 August 1962 Mandela was captured by police who had found his trail. Charged with leaving the country illegally Nelson was convicted and sentenced to five years in prison.

The Rivonia Trial

Mandela was already in prison when South African police discovered the ANC military high command at Liliesleaf Farm. Among the documents that they found was a plan called Operation Mayibuye, which outlined strategy for **guerrilla** warfare in South Africa. This news was political dynamite, and in October Mandela and ten other **activists** – including Walter Sisulu – were charged with **sabotage**.

Chief Luthuli's Nobel Prize and Mandela's own high profile meant that this was going to be a trial like no other in South Africa. The police released elements of what they had found in the Liliesleaf documents, which led to front-page newspaper stories with headlines such as 'Revolution on a military basis'.

Liliesleaf Farm had provided a secluded setting for ANC planning meetings.

The trial, which soon became known as the Rivonia Trial (because that was where most of the evidence had been found), began in October 1963. Mandela, Sisulu and the other **defendants** pleaded 'not guilty' to the charges on the grounds that the state (government) was not based on **democratic** ideals. Lawyers for the state argued that the eleven defendants were dangerous criminals, aiming to overthrow civilized life in South Africa. The stakes were high – a sentence of guilty could lead to the death penalty for all the accused.

The state continued its case until 29 February 1964. The team of lawyers representing the defendants disagreed on whether the eleven should **testify**. Most of the defendants wanted to testify, partly to show that their plans for sabotage were not aimed at injuring people. They believed that the ANC, and all that it stood for, was on trial. With national and international reporters present, the ANC would have a chance to make its case clearly and forcefully. In the end, they decided to testify.

Mandela spoke first, painting a picture of the inequality in South African life and how the ANC plans were not to promote **civil war** but to prepare for it. Walter Sisulu and the others continued this theme. Meanwhile, people held **vigils** in London and elsewhere in support of the defendants.

The trial continued for months until eventually, on 11 June 1964, Mandela and the other main defendants were found guilty. After a terrible night in suspense, the defendants learned that they would be sentenced to life imprisonment.

'I have fought against white domination and I have fought against black domination. I have cherished the ideal of a democratic and free society in which all persons live together in harmony and with equal opportunities. It is an ideal which I hope to live for and to achieve. But if needs be, it is an ideal for which I am prepared to die.'
Nelson Mandela's closing statement at the end of the Rivonia Trial

Mandela was sentenced to life imprisonment and hard labour in Robben Island Prison following his conviction at the Rivonia Treason Trial 1964.

Politics in the 1960s

By the time of the Rivonia Trial the South African government had few friends outside its own borders. Luthuli's Nobel Prize typified the international view of **apartheid** and the United Nations had passed several resolutions condemning the racist form of government. South Africa had turned its back on the **Commonwealth** and was banned from many international organizations, including the Olympic Movement.

Undaunted, the government ploughed ahead with its apartheid philosophy. In the early 1960s Verwoerd took steps to allow the **Bantustans** to become self-governing to some extent. The amount of land set aside for these 'homelands' still amounted to only 13 per cent of South Africa's total – hardly enough to support 75 per cent of the country's population. Through these years the government retained the support of its Afrikaner voting base. If anything, some Afrikaners believed that the government was too lax. In 1966 Prime Minister Verwoerd was assassinated by a white farmer who believed that the government was too 'soft' on the black issue. Verwoerd's successor, Balthazar Vorster, continued the apartheid programme and tightened security even further.

> 'Africans used to get porridge in the morning and evening, and corn in the afternoon. Coloureds and Indians got porridge in the morning, samp [coarsely ground corn porridge] in the afternoon with bread. The quantity of meat was also different. Coloureds and Indians had more than Africans.'
>
> **Ahmed Kathrada, sentenced with Mandela in the Rivonia Trial, describing how Robben Island Prison officials tried to create divisions between prisoners of different backgrounds**

The power of symbols

Everything about the famous Rivonia Trial and its aftermath was tied up with symbolism, which both the South African government and the anti-apartheid movement sought to **exploit**. For the government, the guilty verdict sent a forceful message to those who would oppose apartheid. The convicted men were flown to Robben Island, the notorious prison standing several miles off Cape Town in Table Bay. And even the sentence of life, rather than death, could be viewed as a merciful gesture on the part of a government that proclaimed its own Christian heritage.

The ANC, of course, could present the image of eleven resolute **defendants** sacrificing everything, including their freedom, for a noble cause. And with its senior leadership now either in exile or imprisoned, the ANC wanted its message to resonate – not just internationally, but in the townships and countryside where the struggle would have to continue. While in prison, Mandela and the other ANC men retained their dignity and self-composure, knowing that news of their behaviour would eventually seep past the prison walls. They organized study sessions and debates, so that the harsh prison came to be known as 'the University'.

Turning point: Soweto

During the late 1960s and early 1970s Vorster's government intensified the measures to support **apartheid** by separating and dividing the majority black population. Once more the focus was on the ten **Bantustans**, or 'homelands', which the government saw as the natural place for the different elements of the black population. The Bantu Homelands Constitution Act, passed in 1971, gave the government power to grant self-government to successive Bantustans. Using this legislative route, Ciskei and Bophuthatswana became partly independent in 1972.

Stirrings of freedom

Much to the distaste of the South African government, the international community never recognized the independence of the Bantustans. From the late 1960s, though, South Africa had to contend with the prospect of genuinely independent – and potentially anti-apartheid – neighbours on its doorstep. The first of these countries were a trio that had been under the control of the High Commissioner for South Africa – Swaziland, Lesotho and Botswana. In 1965 these three became independent countries. Swaziland and Lesotho were relatively poor and, more importantly, almost completely dependent on South Africa for their economic well-being. Botswana was a different matter. Larger and more prosperous because of its mineral wealth, this country was able to maintain an independent stance, voicing criticisms of the apartheid regime.

In the early 1970s the two Portuguese **colonies** of Mozambique and Angola were in the throes of **guerrilla** wars as rival factions fought for independence of the colonial power. The Portuguese government fell in 1975, and in the same year Mozambique and Angola became independent. The new governments were actively hostile towards the South African government and offered assistance to the ANC and other anti-apartheid groups. The independence struggles of these two countries provided inspiration for black South Africans.

Against this background of renewed hope there arose a new movement, known as Black Consciousness, in South Africa. With the banning of the ANC and PAC, there was a void to be filled in the powerful anti-apartheid movement. Black Consciousness had similar aims to those of the PAC at its founding but its leaders, notably Steve Biko, believed that the PAC had been thwarted because it had been too impatient. Biko argued that blacks –

Dancers celebrate Botswana's independence in 1965.

and here he included everyone classified as 'non-white' – should take responsibility for their own freedom struggle. The first step was for blacks to liberate themselves from the sense of inferiority that three centuries of white rule had bred. Self-help was the strategy, and the movement set up trust funds for prisoners' families and for black students.

'We are oppressed, not as individuals, not as Zulus, Xhosas, Venda or Indians. We are oppressed because we are black. We must use that concept to unite ourselves and to respond as a cohesive group.'
Steve Biko, outlining Black Consciousness strategy in the early 1970s

Explosion in Soweto

The Black Consciousness message was effective, and by the mid-1970s had become popular among school-age children. Schools in the townships, particularly, were ripe for the message because the Bantu Education system deliberately kept funds low for black schools in urban areas. Under the logic of apartheid, these people had no real rights living in 'white' areas and should really be educated in their respective Bantustans. In addition, the government decided to flex its muscle by insisting that certain subjects, such as mathematics, be taught only in Afrikaans.

This last move, in 1975, prompted an explosion of protest among township schoolchildren. The most important protest was in June 1976 in the township of Soweto (its name is simply an acronym for South West Township), near Johannesburg. In a grisly echo of Sharpeville sixteen years before, police eventually opened fire, killing two young students. Within days the revolt had spread to other townships across South Africa. Young protesters widened the aims of their protest to include shebeens, the illegal drinking houses of the townships. They believed that alcohol broke up families and deadened the resolve of adults to confront **apartheid**. The government responded harshly, using arms in many cases. By the end of the protests, which carried over to 1977, some 575 people had been killed and 3389 wounded. The police rounded up the Black Consciousness leaders and had them tried on the charge of inciting revolution.

The Soweto uprisings of 1976 marked the most violent outbreaks of civil unrest in South Africa's history.

'It was obvious that they regarded us, the Rivonia Trialists, as moderates. After so many years of being branded a radical revolutionary, to be perceived as a moderate was a novel and not altogether pleasant feeling'.
Nelson Mandela recalling the attitude of the first wave of convicted Black Consciousness activists arriving at Robben Island Prison in 1976

Biography – Steve Biko

Stephen Biko (1946–1977) was one of the most powerful players in the long struggle against apartheid. Biko was born in King William's Town, in what is now the province of Eastern Cape. He entered the University of Natal in 1966 to study medicine. He was one of the founders of the Black Consciousness Movement (BCM) in the late 1960s. Students like Biko were the leaders of the BCM and in 1968 they also founded the South African Students' Organization. Biko was a powerful and influential speaker and in 1972 a coalition of more than 70 black organizations established the Black People's Convention, naming Biko the honorary president.

The brutal police treatment of Steve Biko led to his death in 1997, aged only 31.

Biko fought off criticism from the ANC and other anti-apartheid groups that his philosophy excluded whites, but he maintained that the first steps for black liberation had to be made by blacks themselves. Moreover, he argued for non-violent, legal protests at a time when the ANC had set itself on the path of armed struggle. The South African government initially tolerated the BCM, but began cracking down on it in the early 1970s. Biko was banned from many activities in 1973 and arrested several times. In August 1977, in the wake of the turbulence that began in Soweto, Biko was arrested again, manacled and kept naked in a cell for 20 days. Biko was severely beaten by the police while in custody. He lapsed into a coma and died within a month of his arrest.

Media attention

The free exchange of ideas, expressed through the freedom of the press, is an essential element in the working of a **democratic** system. South Africa, during its **apartheid** years, professed to be a democracy but failed to meet the basic test of a democracy: whether the government is truly representative of the people as a whole. South Africa had some of the superficial trappings of a democratic society – such as a British-style parliamentary system based on government by the majority party in Parliament – but it denied voting rights to most of the people living in the country that it governed.

Censorship

A government representing so few of the people will always feel itself to be on the defensive, and in the case of South Africa the government took steps to limit freedom of expression. Apartheid was condemned by many foreign governments and organizations right from the start in 1948, but the South African government took great care to 'shield' South Africans from these views. It also tried to ensure that South Africans would not learn about **dissenting** views within their own country. A systematic apparatus for controlling information developed during the premiership of H F Verwoerd (1958–1966).

A multi-racial group of university students stages a protest at Cape Town University, 1988.

In 1963 the government set up the Publications Control Board. Its role was to check – and ban if necessary – books, periodicals, motion pictures and music. Through the Board, the government tried to ensure that South Africans would remain 'unscathed' by systems of thought that it believed to be immoral. The idea of different races living together was one such notion that needed to be quashed through censorship. Other political sentiments, however, also needed to be screened. And since much of the language of apartheid focused on the moral crusade to stamp out **communism**, anything remotely related to communism was also banned. The interpretation of what exactly constituted communism was, as usual for successive white governments, very hazy.

The news media, mainly radio and newspapers, had to refrain from reporting many events that showed the government in a bad light. Editors and publishers faced heavy fines, and sometimes prison sentences, if they overstepped the mark. As late as the 1980s South African newspapers were banned from printing any photographs of Nelson Mandela or any words that he had ever spoken or written.

Going to absurd lengths

The Publications Control Board had an enormous task in trying to control the total flow of media information reaching South Africans. Because of this overload of work – and also in fear of government reaction if they allowed something 'unacceptable' into the country – the Board preferred to 'play safe' by banning works that most people would agree were perfectly harmless.

One example was the novel Black Beauty, the much-loved children's story about a girl and her horse, which was banned because of its title.

Sneaking works past the Board became something of a sport for many South Africans. A favourite trick for importing 'unacceptable' films was to change the title on the film canister (to something to do with the Bible or perhaps wildlife) and then to add several minutes' worth of such a film to the beginning of the real film. The gamble was that the censor would become bored during these first few minutes and simply rewind the film, allowing it to pass through freely.

The government knew that television would be even more of a threat to censorship, because images of violence – coupled with foreign programmes that would inevitably be imported – would have an enormous effect for change. South Africa resisted introducing television for more than three decades after television broadcasts were launched in most western countries.

International exposure

Foreign journalists based in South Africa also had restrictions – for example, on where they could travel and whom they could interview – but they were able to report events far more freely. Stark images often accompanied stories dealing with watershed events: dead bodies lying face down in Sharpeville in 1960, Steve Biko's corpse in 1977, angry township youths in the wake of the Soweto uprisings.

These stories and images helped bring into focus the nature of the **apartheid** system. They also inspired a range of international measures intended to isolate South Africa in order to bring about an end to apartheid. In 1964, South Africa was banned from the Olympic Games. The United Nations often criticized South Africa and instituted a cultural and sporting **boycott** against the country. Things looked worse for the white government when the United States – the world's economic superpower and the **bulwark** against **communism** – joined these voices of protest.

Anti-apartheid demonstrators came out in force to protest against the 1970 South African cricket tour of England.

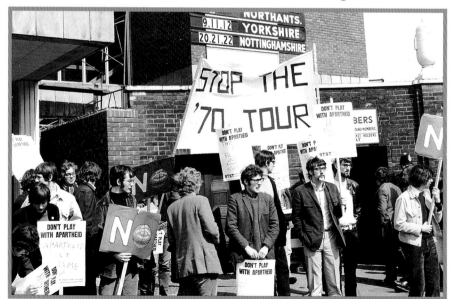

Sun City was one striking example of apartheid in action - a lavish resort where white folk played while the blacks of the surrounding homelands lived in misery and oppression.

In the mid-1980s the National Association for the Advancement of Coloured People (NAACP) campaigned for economic **sanctions** against South Africa. The United States imposed economic sanctions on South Africa in 1986. Hard-nosed companies, not noted for their crusading moral spirit, began to view South Africa as a bad risk and began pulling out of the country.

By the early 1980s much of the foreign interest in South Africa was focused on the man most people saw as the only hope for the country's future – Nelson Mandela. In 1979 Oliver Tambo and other senior ANC officials in Angola had decided on a strategy. The campaign, fuelled by media interest in the man and his history, captured the world's imagination. Streets and squares were renamed in Mandela's honour throughout the world and there also began a concerted campaign for his release from prison. 'Free Nelson Mandela' became a slogan, a song title, the focus of a huge concert and – as a way of going full circle – a headline in the liberal newspaper, the *Johannesburg Sunday Post*, in March 1980. Below the headline was a **petition** people could sign for the release of Mandela and his fellow **political prisoners**. The normal restrictions on reporting and images remained, but the message was staring South Africans in the face.

*'Less than an hour after we had released a statement calling off the **strike**, the government-run South African Broadcasting Corporation (SABC) read our announcement in full. Normally, the SABC ignored the ANC altogether; only in defeat did we make their broadcasts.'*
Nelson Mandela recalling the ANC's cancellation of a general strike in 1958

The power of foreign opinion

The most extreme advocates of **apartheid** believed – or at least hoped – that South Africa could ignore the protests of the outside world. For them, Afrikaners had a religious mission to maintain their own homeland. In their view, South Africa had the natural resources and economic potential to be self-sufficient. How the government maintained power was a matter for themselves, the white minority, to decide. In other words, apartheid was an internal affair, and outsiders had no business trying to 'bully' South Africa into changing its system.

The reality was very different. Most South Africans, including members of successive National Party governments, realized that their country was linked to the outside world and that it could never survive with a complete 'go it alone' stance. This conclusion was not necessarily based on a closer examination of the morality of racial **discrimination**: instead it was based on economics. One single example proves how the government relied on a pragmatic approach in its dealings with the outside world. The gold- and diamond-mining industries had long been a mainstay of the South African economy, and the price of gold, for example, on the world market was linked to South Africa's economic well-being. Controlling the international availability of gold was vital to keeping this price high. In order to do this South Africa had to enter into agreements with the other main gold-producing country, the Soviet Union. Of course the Soviet Union was the leader of world **communism**, the anti-religious political philosophy that successive South African governments had pledged themselves to root out in their own country. But in the end, economic concerns outweighed political rhetoric, and the agreements continued.

But South Africa's economy was far more complex and the country relied on economic links with many other nations. These links ranged from sports and entertainment to manufacturing and farming. If South Africa's trading partners – either individually or collectively – showed their distaste for apartheid by imposing trade **sanctions**, then the economy would really be affected. And media representatives of these major economic powers – including the United States, the United Kingdom, France, Germany and Japan – were based in South Africa, ready to report the latest atrocities or harsh **legislation**.

Apartheid on film

The plight of South Africans living in the apartheid system was never a popular Hollywood subject, perhaps because the truth was so depressing for international audiences. Two notable exceptions were *Cry, the Beloved Country* (1951), based on the novel by the South African anti-apartheid novelist Alan Paton. Towards the end of the apartheid era the American actor Denzel Washington portrayed Steve Biko in the film *Cry Freedom* (1987), which chronicles Biko's friendship with the liberal white newspaper editor Donald Woods.

The campaign to free Nelson Mandela – typified by this 1988 march in Glasgow – became the focus of the international anti-apartheid cause.

Turning point: Mandela's release

By the 1980s the strength of world opinion against **apartheid** was taking effect in South Africa. Foreign companies were pulling out of South Africa, property prices were falling and – an important indicator of the national mood – more whites were leaving South Africa than were entering the country. Prime Minister Vorster's successor, P W Botha, felt forced to bow to the pressure for reform. In 1984 South Africa adopted a new constitution, which provided **parliamentary representation** for coloureds and Indians. Whites would still have the deciding say in Parliament, and there was still no black representation. At the time, this government strategy was described as 'sharing power while retaining control'.

That same year saw the establishment of the United **Democratic** Front (UDF), a broad-based alliance of groups opposed to apartheid. The UDF shared many of the aims that the ANC had adopted at the time of the Freedom Charter (see page 28). Using a combination of intimidation and persuasion, the UDF was able to call a series of **strikes** and **boycotts** of local elections. Violence flared up and the country plunged into a **State of Emergency** in 1986. And although the UDF was banned in 1988, the mineworkers' union declared its **allegiance** to the ANC and called a strike over wages.

Thinking the unthinkable

Prime Minister Botha suffered a stroke in 1989 and was replaced by F W de Klerk, who at first seemed prepared to continue the hard-line stance of Botha and previous National Party leaders. Botha, despite his stroke, retained the office of President until de Klerk was elected to that post in an election in August 1989.

One of de Klerk's first moves as President was to order the release from prison of several leading ANC figures, notably Walter Sisulu and Govan Mbeki, the oldest of the Rivonia trialists. They were not given **banning orders** and were allowed to speak legally as ANC representatives. President de Klerk continued to make improvements by removing many of the restrictions imposed by apartheid. The President and his allies in the higher ranks of the National Party felt that the only way to preserve the status quo was to increase government repression and violence against the majority population. This tactic might buy another ten years of pure power, but would undoubtedly lead to a violent reaction when they did lose power.

The National Party was, in effect, trying to reduce the pressure by according the ANC more freedom. Also, the late 1980s saw the downfall of **communism** in Europe and with it went one of the major cornerstones of apartheid strategy – containing the menace of communism.

High-level bargaining

Even during the leadership of P W Botha, the Free Mandela campaign had had a great effect. In 1989 Botha had invited Mandela to a secret meeting, hoping to persuade the ANC leader to abandon violence. Mandela would not agree – and Botha, for his part, would not agree to classify ANC inmates as **political prisoners** – but the stage had been set for further meetings.

With the release of Sisulu and other ANC leaders, Mandela sensed that de Klerk seriously wanted change and met him on 13 December 1989. The president listened carefully as the prospect of Mandela's release came up. Mandela pointed out that even if he were released he would have to be rearrested immediately if the ANC remained an illegal organization. On 2 February 1990 President de Klerk addressed the South African Parliament and made several dramatic announcements. He was to lift the bans on the ANC and 33 other organizations; he would free all political prisoners not convicted of violence; he would end **capital punishment**; and he would lift many other restrictions. 'The time for negotiation has arrived', he said.

The Nelson Mandela who returned to freedom in 1990 was vigorous and energetic – an ideal symbol of his country's democratic hopes.

President Mandela

The biggest news, of course, came when Nelson Mandela emerged as a free man on 11 February 1990. The release was a joyous occasion and was re-enacted on a less grand scale as other ANC prisoners were released or as exiles were able to return legally to their own country. However, not everyone in de Klerk's party was as forward-thinking as the National Party leader. They were not prepared to give in to majority rule, particularly to an opponent (the ANC) that had not abandoned its armed struggle. (The ANC had not been responsible for many deaths, but it still retained its official support for violent measures if necessary.) ANC supporters, at the same time, wanted a wholesale change immediately. And adding to the confusion was the threat that the mainly Zulu Inkatha Freedom Party might **boycott** any elections unless they were promised some sort of **autonomy**.

It was only after prolonged negotiations between the government and the ANC that some sort of agreement could be reached. Finally, on 13 November 1993 the two sides agreed to institute a non-racial, non-sexist, unified and **democratic** South Africa based on the principle of 'one person, one vote'. The first genuine national election in South Africa was held in April 1994 and the ANC won a decisive victory. On 10 May 1994 Nelson Mandela was inaugurated as president of this new South Africa.

Archbishop Desmond Tutu, seen here with Nelson Mandela in 1990, had played a high-profile part in the negotiations to end apartheid.

Biography – F W de Klerk

Frederik Willem de Klerk was born in Johannesburg and earned a law degree from Potchefstroom University in 1958. He was elected to parliament in 1972 for the National Party and later held a number of cabinet posts before succeeding P W Botha as South Africa's president in August 1989.

Two years after releasing Nelson Mandela and other leading ANC members, de Klerk's government repealed the last of the laws that formed the legal basis of **apartheid**. In March 1992 more than two-thirds of the voters in a whites-only referendum approved his policy of negotiating a new constitution to extend political rights to blacks. He and Mandela were jointly awarded the Nobel Peace Prize in 1993 for negotiating the country's transition to a non-racial democracy.

After losing the presidency to Mandela in 1994, de Klerk continued to serve in the government as one of two deputy presidents until 1996. On 9 May 1996 de Klerk announced that he would establish the National Party as a formal opposition party.

F W de Klerk travelled the country during his failed campaign to retain the presidency in 1994.

Healing the wounds

South Africa entered its new post-**apartheid** era with the good wishes of the world, as well as a surprisingly supportive mood among its own white population. Nevertheless, the job of governing South Africa is not an easy one, and Nelson Mandela faced many difficulties from the start. One of his most important concerns was to make sure that the white population did not flee the country, fearing that the black majority would mount revenge attacks for all the past events under apartheid. He included people of all races in his **cabinet**, and went to great lengths to show that South Africa is – and should remain – the mother country to all who live there. Nelson Mandela and F W de Klerk had shared the 1993 Nobel Peace Prize, and as president, Mandela tried to enlist the support of de Klerk in many political moves. Mandela's government began to tackle the many legacies of inequality – in the fields of education, health, housing and employment.

One of the first issues that Nelson Mandela addressed soon after his release – and which he focused on as president – was the problem of violence. Crime has always been a concern in the country, and it did not disappear overnight when free elections were held. Under President Mandela the South African police force had to change its character: instead of enforcing apartheid it had to concentrate on crime. The majority in the country can now respect the police but violence remains a concern for all South Africans.

Chief Mangosuthu Buthelezi led many Zulu protests over the 1994 elections, at times threatening to disturb South Africa's new-found democracy.

There was another problem, this time from other black groups. The Zulu people, who represent a large portion of the South African population, had long believed that their territory did not have enough **autonomy**. They continued to make this complaint after the 1994 election and their main political party, the Inkatha Freedom Party, even abandoned its seats in Parliament because of these disagreements.

Symbols and succession

In order to tackle the many problems facing South Africa Nelson Mandela needed to play on his role as father figure and peace-maker. For black South Africans, as well as coloureds and Asians, this role was clearly defined. But, to many people's surprise, white South Africans also showed an enormous sense of pride in their new president. For many decades considered outcasts in the view of the outside world, white South Africans could now feel part of a country that had won the world's admiration. Mandela was keen to acknowledge this affection. One lasting image of this new attitude was President Mandela's joining the joyful celebrations following South Africa's victory in the 1995 Rugby World Cup. Rugby had traditionally been a white – and more specifically, an Afrikaner – sport, and to have the country's black president on hand seemed to signal how much things had changed.

When Nelson Mandela turned eighty years old in July 1998 he announced that he would be stepping down as president when his term of office ended in 1999. He knew that he was too old to tackle the difficult day-to-day responsibilities of government. He also recalled how he, along with Walter Sisulu, Oliver Tambo and other young ANC members, had been impatient with the 'old' leadership of their organization some fifty years before. Mandela did not want to stand in the way of the new generation of South African leaders taking the country into the new millennium.

The ANC chose a bright young politician, Thabo Mbeki, to replace him as ANC leader. Mandela had become a political father figure to Mbeki who, as vice-president, had seen first-hand how the government operates. He gave his full support to the ANC, and Mbeki, in the 1999 elections. The ANC won these elections, and in May 1999 Mandela stood down as president and made way for Thabo Mbeki.

The Truth and Reconciliation Commission

Soon after being elected president in 1994, Nelson Mandela set about one of the most important tasks he had ever faced – trying to change attitudes of hatred, bitterness and racism and to begin a time of healing in his country. In May 1994 he established the Truth and **Reconciliation** Commission (TRC), with the well-respected anti-**apartheid** campaigner Archbishop Desmond Tutu at its head. The TRC would hear the testimony of those who had committed acts of violence during the apartheid era, as well as the testimony of those who suffered. The violence and brutality under the spotlight was not just that of the former white government, but of rival black groups who had terrorized the townships during the late 1970s and 1980s.

The TRC decided that those who admitted to committing political crimes would be offered an **amnesty** but that those who remained silent would be prosecuted. Although many people believe that the TRC has helped 'clear the air' in South Africa, it has also been the subject of some disagreement. It is hard for the families of many victims to see the perpetrators of violence walk free. Also, there is a widespread concern that instead of concentrating on the senior members of the white government and security forces who were responsible for devising the strategy of apartheid, the TRC would only be able to deal with those lower down the scale who implemented the strategy.

'We must face the ghastly past and not pretend it never happened, and face up to the beast. And then, shut the door and say we are going to move together into the glorious future.'
Archbishop Desmond Tutu, outlining the aims of the Truth and Reconciliation Commission

Archbishop Desmond Tutu of the TRC encourages Nelson Mandela's ex-wife Winnie to admit to her own wrong-doings during the apartheid years.

Measuring the cost of apartheid

Apartheid took its toll on all of South Africa in many ways. One of the few ways of measuring its effects, however, is by examining some stark economic figures. These indicate exactly how the system deprived the majority of South Africans of a chance for a decent way of life. In the 1970s, the richest 20 per cent of the South African population (by definition almost all white) owned 75 per cent of the country's wealth. By comparison, the same top level of Americans owned less than 40 per cent of US wealth. Using this and other measures of wealth distribution, South Africa had the highest level of wealth inequality in any of the 57 countries worldwide in which such information is available.

'As it is now, they are simply forcing it [the TRC system of amnesty for those who confess] down our throats, and that is what we're objecting to. We are saying justice must be done more, especially when we've got a government that we've waited more than ten years to take action against the criminals.'
Churchill Mxenge, whose brother and sister-in-law were killed by security officers of the former regime

'I understand that forgiveness does not come cheaply. It's something that comes from the heart. And I can just ask the people that were involved directly and indirectly, and were affected by this case, to consider forgiving me.'
Former Police Captain Brian Mitchell, whose 30-year sentence for eleven charges of murder was set aside by the TRC

The New South Africa

South Africa has entered the new millennium with a new constitution guaranteeing fundamental rights to all citizens of the country. The voting system, which had been distorted during the **apartheid** era, has been transformed so that the government is truly representative of the country. And with the Truth and Reconciliation Commission, coupled with the judicial system, aiming to redress past wrongs, it would seem that the fight against apartheid has been won.

Linked to these important breakthroughs in the social arena are a number of advances in the fields of economics and international politics. New companies are investing in South Africa and the economy is growing – at a faster rate than the rise in population. On the international front, South Africa has flexed its muscle, in diplomatic terms, to promote stability in neighbouring states such as Swaziland and Lesotho, as well as in the Democratic Republic of Congo (formerly Zaire), which is recovering from decades of misrule and **civil war**.

Causes for concern

Despite all the progress in less than a decade since the first free elections, there are still important reasons for concern about the future of South Africa. The Zulu discontent, which still smoulders in KwaZulu-Natal, could flare up and spread through the country. The problem of crime, and its associated violence, is still acute and Johannesburg regularly figures as one of the world's most violent cities. And running through the country is a sense of impatience on the part of many black South Africans, who are frustrated by what they see as the slow rate of change.

South Africa need only look to one of its northern neighbours, Zimbabwe, to see how optimism can turn to despair. Zimbabwe, a former British **colony** and later ruled by a white minority (like South Africa), became a fully independent, **democratic** country in 1980. Since that time, however, it has embarked on badly thought out economic policies which have wasted many of the country's natural resources. In response to deteriorating economic conditions, President Robert Mugabe's ZANU-PF party has singled out white farmers as the root of the problem, turning a blind eye as mobs burn farms and attack their white owners. Political opposition has been weakened and many people are fleeing the country.

South Africa finds it hard to shake off its violent past – armed guards are a common sight at many public events such as this soccer game.

As an object lesson for South Africa, the Zimbabwean experience is stark, and the South African government has been observing events to the north closely. South Africa, if it is not to repeat these mistakes, must ensure that its most precious natural resource – its people, of whatever colour – stand behind the government in order to make its transformation permanent.

'I ... extend heartfelt congratulations to all our people, regardless of race, colour and gender, for the extraordinary and sustained effort over the last ten years which has enabled the overwhelming majority among us to say – we are proud to be South African!'
Thabo Mbeki, President of South Africa, February 2000

59

Appendix
South African timeline

1000–1800   Gradual movement of Bantu speakers southwards into present-day south Africa

1487   Portuguese sailors become first Europeans to land near the Cape

1652   First Dutch settlement established in the Cape

1688   Two hundred Huguenots arrive in the Cape, escaping religious persecution in France

1795   Great Britain first occupies the Cape

1809   British administration introduces the first 'pass laws' controlling movement of black people in the Cape

1836   Six thousand Afrikaners set off on the Great Trek, to escape British rule

1860   Labourers brought in from India to work Natal sugar plantations

1867   First diamonds discovered

1886   First big gold mines developed

1899–1902   Boer War (between Afrikaners and British)

1910   Union of South Africa established, with Louis Botha as first prime minister

1912   South African Native National Congress/SANNC (later the African National Congress/ANC) formed

1913   Native Land Act sets aside 7.3 per cent of land for African 'reserves'

1914   National Party established

1934   United Party formed

1948   National Party wins the 'apartheid election'

1940s–early 1950s   Series of acts establish framework of apartheid

1955   Congress of the People drafts the Freedom Charter

1960   Sharpeville Massacre

1961   Albert Luthuli is awarded the Nobel Peace Prize

1964   Nelson Mandela and other ANC leaders sentenced to life imprisonment on charges of sabotage

1976–77   Soweto uprising (against the imposition of Afrikaans in education) spreads through townships

1977   Steve Biko dies in police custody

1986   Prime Minister P W Botha imposes a State of Emergency after violence breaks out

1989   F W de Klerk succeeds Botha; releases ANC Secretary-General Walter Sisulu

1990   Nelson Mandela released; ANC and 32 other opposition groups legalized

1991   Most remaining apartheid legislation abolished

1994   Nelson Mandela elected president in the first free elections in South African history

1999   Thabo Mbeki succeeds Nelson Mandela as president

Suggested reading

Apartheid: a History, by B Lapping – London: Paladin, 1988
The Apartheid Handbook, by R Ormond – London: Penguin, 1987
A Concise History of South Africa, by Robert Ross – Cambridge: Cambridge University Press, 1999
Country Studies: South Africa, by Garrett Nagle – Oxford: Heinemann Library, 1998
Heinemann Profiles: Nelson Mandela, by Sean Connolly – Oxford: Heinemann Library, 1998
I write what I like, by Steve Biko – Oxford: Heinemann, 1979
Long Walk to Freedom, by Nelson Mandela – London: Little, Brown, 1994
My Traitor's Heart, by R Malan – Oxford: Bodley Head, 1990
South Africa: Reform or Revolution? by Allan Leas – London: B T Blatsford, 1992

Useful websites

http://www.UN.org
The main United Nations website has many links to events over the last 50 years in South Africa, including UN resolutions about sanctions, boycotts and South Africa's role in neighbouring states, notably Namibia.

http://www.cnn.com/almanac
This site, operated by the cable television news network CNN, provides information on international events, with many links to events in South Africa – both historical and current.

http://www.beyondracism.org
The site of the Comparative Human Relations Initiative. It is a collaboration among people from Brazil, South America and the United States tackling discrimination and inequality.

http://www.truth.org.za
This is the official site of the Truth and Reconciliation Commission, with a useful mission statement outlining the TRC's aims and also containing testimony of the hundreds of people who have testified before it.

http://www.anc.org.za
The website of the ANC, the majority party in South Africa's government. It provides up to date news and facts about the ANC, the president and useful background information, speeches and history.

http://www.polity.org.za
This site contains wide-ranging information about South Africa's government and constitution.

Glossary

activism, activists vigorous campaigning by people (activists) to bring about social or political change

allegiance loyalty to a ruler or government

amnesty an official pardon

annex to absorb territory into borders of a country or city

antagonism angry behaviour, which can become violent

apartheid a system of segregation and discrimination that made whites and blacks live apart from each other

autonomy possession of, or right to, self-government

banning order government document that limits where someone can go as well as what they can do

Bantustan an area set aside for black people within South Africa to remove them from white-only areas

boycott to avoid dealing with a company, service or even a country in order to force them to change

breechloader a single-shot rifle

bulwark something or someone who stands firm

cabinet the closest advisors to a political leader, who help govern a country

capital punishment the death sentence

civil disobedience protesting against unfair laws by legal means such as marches and demonstrations

civil war a war between two or more groups within the same country

Cold War the period of political hostility from 1945 to 1990 between the United States and its allies and the Soviet Union and its communist allies

colony a region that is ruled by a powerful foreign country

Commonwealth a group of independent countries which had once been ruled by the UK and which promote economic and cultural links among themselves

communism, communist a system of rule that calls for government ownership of property and companies

concentration camp a place where prisoners are kept under strict control

constituency a political area division that elects a representative to parliament or a similar body

constitutional operating within accepted limits of the law

defendant in a trial, a person charged with a crime

democratic describing a political system that allows all people an equal say in how they are governed

dissenting disagreeing with a prevailing view or official decision

discrimination treating individuals or groups in an unequal manner

dominion a self-governing territory belonging to foreign sovereign or government

elite a minority that has an advantage, in terms of wealth or political power

emulate follow the example of

exploit to gain advantage from something

franchise in politics, the legal right to vote in elections

guerrilla fighting in small armed bands, as opposed to large armies

intern to imprison someone without a trial

legislation laws, considered collectively

missionary a person or group that goes to another country to try to convert local people to a different (usually Christian) set of beliefs

parliamentary representation the right to elect someone to parliament, or a similar body

persecution prolonged, organized, hostile and harsh behaviour towards an individual or group

petition to make a plea to a ruling body, usually with a document (also called a petition) signed by many people

political prisoner someone who is imprisoned because of his or her political beliefs rather than a crime committed

potent very powerful

reconciliation a restoration of harmony after a period of conflict

sabotage the deliberate destruction of things for a political reason

sanctions economic measures, such as a stoppage of trade, to persuade a country to change its policies

savannah a large, grassy plain in Africa with few trees but dotted with smaller shrubs and bushes

share-cropping farming on someone else's land, and paying the landowner a portion of the crop as rent

squat to occupy land or a building without owning it

State of Emergency a time when many rights (such as free speech) are withdrawn because a government fears violence

strike a stoppage of work by employees in order to press for changes in pay or working conditions

suspended sentence a criminal sentence that is spent away from prison but under observation

tariff a tax paid on goods shipped into a region

testify to make a statement in court

vigil a long period of time that people spend together to show support for someone or something

white supremacy a racist concept that whites are better than black, coloured or Asian peoples

Index